blue jeaned buddhists

poetry by
dan jacoby

Copyright © 2019 Dan Jacoby

All rights reserved. No part of this book may be reproduced or distributed in any form without prior written permission from the publisher.

The publisher hereby grants permission to reviewers and scholars to use brief quotations. Please direct any questions and/or notices of reviews to ducklakebooks@gmail.com.

blue jeaned buddhists: Paperback Edition

Manufactured in the United States of America

ISBN: 978-1-943900-22-0

Library of Congress Control Number: :2019945998

Ocean Shores, Washington, USA
Duck Lake Books
www.ducklakebooks.com

Some poems from *blue jeaned buddhists* have appeared in the following publications: *Ascent Aspirations Magazine, American Journal of Poetry, Canary, Belle Reve Literary Journal, Black Heart Magazine, Bombay Gin, Burningword Literary Journal, Clockwise Cat ,Concho River Review, Cowboy Poetry Press, Dead Flowers-A Rag, Deep South Magazine, Euphony, Fishfood Arts and Literary Magazine, Haunted Waters Press, Indiana Journal Review, Lines and Stars, Maudlin House, The Opiate, Pyrokinection, Ragweed Literary Magazine, Red Booth Review, Red Fez ,R.KV.R.Y., Shot Glass Journal, Southwestern American Literature, Steel Toe Review, Tipton Poetry Journal, Tishman Review, Triggerfish Critical Review, The Vehicle,* and *Wilderness House Literary Review.*

contents   blue jeaned Buddhists

a gangbangers wake	1
ageing	2
apology	3
bathroom spider	5
bayou mist	6
blood moon	7
buckaroo	8
cold harbor	9
cross	11
crystal child	12
dogs	13
dead canary	14
driftwood	15
fading sight	16
eleventh commandment	17
ewing avenue	18
in the dark	19
knight rails	20
boston marathon	22
mark the time	23
mirrors	24
no real fear	26
nobody	27

of the people for the people…	28
william burrough's ghost	29
overtaken	31
presumptive diva	32
proof reading	33
grievances	34
undergraduates	35
reading of the rig veda	36
silent drums	38
sports writers	39
spring 1968	40
teacher	41
tweet from your bones	42
lake ponchartrain 1968	44
white power	45
marijuana dream	46
exercise yard	47
veterans day	48
West Pine Alumni	49
gravity	50
hurricane	51
making music	52
maycomb	53
millennials	55

moon in a henri rousseau painting	56
muse	57
national anthem	58
normal heart	59
on returning to saint louis	61
paradox	62
parmita dana (perfection of clarity)	64
pencil sharpener	65
student loans	66
PTSD	67
scout lee	68
sleeping sycamores	69
south side hardware	70
suicide at owl creek farm	71
synthesis	72
terry pratt	73
tomahawk	75
troubadour	77
waiting on a roller coaster	79
Waste Hauler	81
water woman	82
william faulkner's rocking chair	83
About the Poet	85

blue jeaned buddhists

For Pat, Kate and Liz

(Chicago, 1974, 102nd and Halsted)

A gangbanger' wake

boy almost seventeen
buried on his birthday
lay in his coffin
in deaths wake they
sat him up God
and shot him five more
times in the black
back waters
his mother weeps
conceiving

ageing

sometimes at the end of the day
just before giving up on waking
trying to gather thoughts
about the next day
failures, victories
like a preening tom cat
going over old ground
listening for a sound, a chance
to minister some resolution
a figment like green, gatsby, beacon
fresh to the scent
daises and coke bottle glasses
found in barbwire hardened wastes
hear the house move
just so in a dharma wind
cat hears it too
he hears much more
ears still ringing
from a 1970's firebase shelling
back cramping, flinching
feel my heart racing
sensing an incoming old terror
mind no longer in neutral

apology

at seventy-two it's harder to see
in gray light of a cloudy dawn
birds were farther away than I thought
at least sixty yards not thirty
the mallards flair as I swing to shoot
two pair climbing over buck brush
highballing with the wind
toward the west into Hindle bottoms
retreating to the back of the blind
I watch them become pepper specks
chastising myself out loud for my hurry,
levee I hide on once protected forty acres
of well tended high yield corn fields
now a landscape transformed by bulldozers
not truly wilderness of my ancestors
farmers from nassau region on rhine river
who struggled in clearing this land for planting

looking through cut willows
I estimate the distance to farthest decoy to be forty yards
scanning mottled late fall clouds for more redlegs
not like the days of my childhood with dad
thousands of birds would come like a whirling storm
drifting down into bobbing decoys
like the release of leaves in the fall
sky would be black with the weight of relentless migration
teal, golden eye, pintail, mallards, woodies, and grebes
looking up from my memories there are four sprigs
the distance is feet not yards
wings set, feet down, threatening to land in the blind
shooting as I rise two drakes tumble into the blocks
the explosion of the shotgun startles me,
causes hundreds of birds hiding in the buckbrush

to rise madly in unison from wind blown rippling lake
breaking in every direction but mine
the magic spell of that holy place broken
I find myself almost needing to apologize

bathroom spider

in that picture frame
one with pressed flowers
bottom left hand corner
lurks a white spider
kind found
full in summer willows
dangling from fine velvet films
kind that gives red welts
all over pulsing
itching shivering
hides in the white border
singing sad siren songs
seducing loopy winter moths
visiting box elder bug, they
hang like cadaverous fruit,
baroque sunlit christmas ornaments,
abandoned semaphores,
shadow bones
in the shower mist

bayou mist

bottle of bourbon
from old dream alleys
full of hitchhiking navajos
wrapped in sad serapes
carrying worried switchblades
on old boxcar night eyes tearing
leaking like third floor tenement toilets
sitting with nighthawks at three in the morning
in an all night Cajun greasy spoon
passing it through the garden of good and evil
taking a rainy cab ride to the bayou
with a tigress with deceiving shirley temple eyes
sad face ruffle laden lady
people with glitter in their stares
looking with that dharma vision
in pink, red, hurricane glasses
rain still falling, dripping
from kudzu on canal street
locals hang in dark drowsy doorways
like unbalanced buddhist prayer wheels
starving dogs loiter at dumpsters
or lay dead in gutters
waiting for the storm out at sea
howling a warning surrounding
these languishing lost mad hobos
alcohol is for the pain of memory
creates a movie in their minds
that crashes down like the oncoming storm
hoping that lighting a devotional candle
at preservation hall will chase the demons
as I open the bourbon and look
for a bottle of canada dry

blood moon

early this morning
before an autumn dawn
frost as yet a no show
in crisp low october fog
dogs give me long looks
questioning faces
you're never up this early
old man in house slippers
grass is dew thick
getting in where laces once were
peacocks hear dogs
call out an alarm
grey scattered clouds
like fish scales form
stars flow across sky
hurrying westward
like traffic on a french boulevard
many centuries have past
this moon observed such
how many are left to me
a thing I'll never know
like looking at comedy and death
with the same expression

buckaroo

in the 1860's
men had meaningful gunfights
not the fast draw kind
no, they shot each other
in bars, whore houses, alleys
usually in the back
west's version of the drive by
nothing changes
guns now have magazines
with more issues
than the new yorker
fired quickly more effectively
young men get killed still
by guns with foreign names
in the back, running away
hands in the air, tickets punched
bushwhacked

*(nominated for a Pushcart Prize by
Tipton Poetry Journal for 2015)*

cold harbor

all symbols of hate
these stars
these blue bars
of bravery
history opines
these men died
not the old
architects of this slaughter
seven thousand fell at cold harbor
in just twenty minutes
soldiers grey and blue
wonder at the sacrifice
for lack of compromise

conversations between pickets
night before battle engaged
sharing of coffee, water, hardtack
sharing stories of battle, home
killing each other
very next day
what matter the Cause to them
following their states to ruin
following melville's meteor
to the grave

eighty some years after
penning a bill of rights
colonial ties and slavery
pulled many a state's flowers asunder
where was god then
northern arrogance
southern truculence
their honor, memory

sullied by future sins
fueled of hate and greed
gaze at the graves
arlington, chickamaugua, gettysburg, shiloh
only there is heard
whispers of conscience
of futile prayer
not to forget the lesson
not to disregard the anguish
swords cracked
bayonets broken
bloody angle, pickets charge, the cornfield
assault on fort wagner
our remarkable blindness

mothers, daughters, fathers, sons
torn to pieces
healing no where in sight
of nationalism, sectionalism
grind a ghoulish agenda
bugling another charge
to oblivion
like a gothic sketch
dotted with crosses, headstones
with those left standing
in hell's maelstrom
and darkness of hate

cross

third day of a seven day binge
party line is
take him to confession
kind of….sometimes…..maybe
faith's last stand
up for the down stroke
need for adrenalin rush
to elevate the moment
mistake not to engage others
should run towards that shit
breathe in new long vowels
into some old words
come up with new nickname
stop surfing underground
old boots in new dirt
heading for newtown beach
to pull the sea air over him
and soak off
all the old mattress labels

crystal child
        (for Richard 4 July 2014)

childhood was one
beating after another
so bad, loaded single shot
twenty eight gauge
going to kill him
didn't come back
skull crushed crashing
Harley, above right eye
lost everything, brother first,
his mind, never had anything
made living making things
most found no value in

loss and failure
created maniacal paranoia-
always armed in bars,
parties, picnics
spent many new year's eve
in cahokia gripping 20 gauge ithaca
only daughter fights men
in dark alton bars tattooed and
undefeated to this day

moved from ghetto violence
to quiet country town
where fathers beat sons
with shovels, axe handles
on twelve hundred a month
slowly going mad with anxiety
had to make a history up
to battle life of rendering
the stink of catatonic loneliness
to simple carnie arcade game

dogs

standing on corner
under glowing street lights
at sixty-third and menard
old Italian man
in knee length, white apron
selling dirty water hot dogs
faded blue work shirt
buttoned at the neck
baggy grey pants that
tumbled over his worn tom mc cans
tattered friday hat
pulled just to heavy eyebrows
spoke with old world accent
mustard spread with wood sticks
piled onions and sweet green relish high
quickly but carefully wrapped
in white butcher paper
each stacked like soldiers
in a tall brown sack
every night of summer
in my youth he was there
until I went off to war
some fifty years later
eat my dogs the same way

dead canary

hard working this actor
shows up everywhere
wild eyed charisma
everything a production
worth watching
like a canary
in a coal mine
irish call him a "mixer"
alone in a bar for a moment
soon philosophizing with regulars
about shakespeare's dealing with mortality
in midsummers night dream
covers punk rock or duke ellington
came out of southie
ex roadie for whalen jennings
ran for office in college
by throwing keg parties
seems always running for mayor
uses a rectal thermometer
to check popularity level
preserving the mantle of sanity
never accepting that
his ticket was never punched
believes in his own karma
rolling with it
like an urban buddhist
never taking his boot
off the neck of life
for fear that it will get up
and walk away

driftwood

braced against this morning chill
some driftwood feeds my fire
on dry creek bank
bare from late fall flood
water is still, cold, deep, and dark
now in the fog
above the crackling fire
young man comes with plastic jugs
long lines attached to hooks
he will spend day fishing on the creek bottom
for mudcat and carp
he will soon be in prayer as
his weighted baited jars
float silently patiently

in the still world
i would greet him
surely he would sit
spell out weather wisdom
warm himself to foxfire lore
but I don't for some reason
moves on hands in heavy gloves
I return to myself as
wind plays havoc with the blaze
in minutes crows discover the fisherman
trees of full flapping magpie critics
will look over his shoulder all day
hoping he will drop some liver bait
having second thoughts, douse the fire
walking after him like a blue jeaned buddhist

fading sight

> *"and then I could not see"*
> *Emily Dickinson*

fly on the screen
bounces on surface
doing a frenetic tango
in the smoke of my cigar
in panic mode to escape
james taylor seems to soothe
poor beastie

same one that bit me earlier
ponder to help his exit
to the outer world
or the next
its' eggs appear specs
on the white walls
mercy promises
more in kind

it lands on the dog at my feet
dog takes little notice
shiver sends it on it's way
back to the light
confused desperate
tomorrow will be legs up
on the dusty sill

or will it be as
dickinson described so aptly
the very last
I see

eleventh commandment

group looking for help,
see, the bible, well,
not quite conservative enough
want to rewrite it too
fit their narrow view to bale
maybe jack hammer in there
eleventh special commandment begetting
hate speech and helicopter morality
and maybe defending just jim crow
and white bred bland santa and
the baby freaking, jesus, christmas
and damning all to democratic hell
that question the third great awakening
being held in the almighty's hands
over a fiery barbecue pit mindless
preaching of the great exclusivity
of their brand of anti damn everything
while claiming martyr like persecution
some camouflaged mobile aristocracy
who marry camels and frogs
and claiming loudly that on some sixth day
never being any good with numbers
your god created man then murder
in his own miserable image
of self-fulfilling prophecy

ewing avenue

loved to watch puerto rican girls
tattooed mexican girls
with black painted lips
with cigarettes, high hair
walking, hands on hips
pointed straight down to the grey pavement
swaying to piped out bodega music
on ewing avenue

addicts running up to cars
offering to rag wash windshields
begging for money in the bush
connected families
sitting the stoops
like it was their religious duty
cerveza rubia in hand
smell of hemp in the air
on humid summer nights
mellow mariachi music
a fiesta de quinceanera

marred by gunfire
terror driven drive-bys
vibrant flowering life succumbs
like an over tightened piano wire
to the stranglehold of poverty
gangbangers who claim pretentiously
to be kings

in the dark
> "...grandfather night in this old house scares me
> with its' black coffin.."
> Jack Kerouac

we are just soldiers
dance floor cowboys
bare ass naked
on the floor with strangers
more will follow if we go down

like artic monkeys
under a black hole sun
we disappear for a while
and turn up as someone else
in a woody allen movie

world was built by killers
in dive bar t shirts
bathed in 13.4 billion year old starlight
shadows forced out of corners
pouring out like the sea

we become wild cards
that don't give a shit
new fast fading versions
voices hidden
in tangled holiday lights

now to a ninja beat
of the n train to coney island
roommates of a fierce cosmic funk
we have become that someone
who left us in the dark

knight rails

late monday evening
in san jose yards
waiting for the 4:30 zipper
if that failed
the ghost at midnight
switchmen warned of the yard bull
violent malevolent cruel
boarded ghost east of yards
got off to avoid search in watsonville
hid in weeds until the highball
slept away the night
rolling down the coast to
city of angels
being put to sleep
by crashing of ocean waves
at 60 miles an hour

washed hair and face
with melt water
from reefer car baptismal font
30 mile bus ride to riverside
escaping coast's smog blanket
slept on a dry river bed
like a chinese priest
under navajo stars
warmed by a two grey hills blanket
daybreak on a santé fe freight
bound for st. louis

america rolls by through dark mountains
across brown winter plains
where emptiness is discrimination
nothing is lost to the eye

on a well worn path
like watching a dog's paw twitch
in the buffalo grass while it dreams
driving secret of existence, sampatei,
devoid of any wrong predicates
a vast empty chalk board
erased, rewritten, erased again
with each new day, new life
no alternatives

boston marathon

on a road, race
dead age doing what
it does best, run
while thunder sounds
wrapped in stubborn oak-
the tree already
in his house plays
at being secure
while hurricane voices
sing Christmas carols
on Boston Green-
blind endeavor to truth;
a proof of something brave
safely hauntingly hidden
a near miss
struggling to survive
no compromise at the finish

mark the time

high blue azure sky
so clear today
not even a contrail
carp striking at the surface
at cobwebs wind blown from trees
so many breaking through the cover
looks like skipping rocks
cranes flit about searching
for fish and fresh water clams
bobcat screeches off to the south
resents my being here
winter sun reflects off unfrozen lake
blinding my southern view
blackbirds in no particular hurry
pass in a catatonic flight pattern
yapping at each other
large buck passes quietly on north bank
followed by a doe with twins
wary mallards land off in buck brush
while five hooded mergansers
dance in the decoys
sundown's timber shadows
creep across the muddy lake
like ancient spirits of Sauk and Fox
draw with the wind
a myriad of patterns
on the brown water easel
for a few fleeting seconds
erase it and start again
off to the west high stratus fingers
reach to the darkening east
cold front crawling bringing winter
even the eagles absent today
with the scent of snow in the air

mirrors

golden age superstition
mirror's reflection captured
parts of one's soul
if broken, damages soul
of one who broke it

death the in home meant covering
mirrors in purple
preventing a soul from
being trapped within,
children told sternly
avoid looking too deeply
theirs could be captured completely

still a phobia
one approaches reflections cautiously
seeking approval
like the queen
in sleeping beauty
fearing what it contains

some, see what they want
others, shun revelation
we are what we are
until we hide the flaws
desiring to project image
impress the world
be accepted

crisp shiny bathroom mirrors
allow to probe deeply
flaws of age, worry, crisis
hardly noticed in others

tends to complicate lives
rather than bare answers

fascination with self
causes storing of likenesses
forcing the inevitable
hour glass of civilization
creates so many different portraits
clarification becomes clouded
self worth deluded

before there were mirrors
artists painted and waters reflected
images that we needed help to see
early man must have gazed quizzically
in pools of eddying water
wondering at what it was
thinking reflection not his own
but a creature of the dark water
today, we dwell on image
over the length of the day
over a life time, and finally
in the hands of the reaper

no real fear

coffee is good this morning
rained hard for two days now
just starting to let up
wind is getting up
it will get colder
every season has a day
when it folds into the next
today is that day
most of the leaves fallen
squirrels in panic mode, gathering
birds five deep at feeders
smell of snow not quite in the air
ponds and lakes will soon freeze
thanksgiving five days away
now timber scent is heavy
the very earth gives off
inherent primordial pheromones
reminder of our origin, our future
somehow peaceful feeling
of unknown anticipation
with no real fear

nobody

memories of childhood
remain forever close
full recall at any moment,
peggy telling you in fifth grade
she can no longer be your girlfriend,
many times family had to move
suffered through many first days at school
mother's failed boy friends
tables bused to pay rent
remember those not seen in thirty years
pick up a conversation ended in high school
grew up in prison town with a college
small time eight ball hustler
parents split when he was nine
had dad's outlaw streak
took a few years to realize
was a nobody from nowhere
no summer camps, disney vacations
just a kid from the irish channel
dropped out of college
betting more on the ethereal
worked texas oil rigs
read russian novels
associated with loose coalition of freaks-
anti-social punks who
just wanted to live
goes back to a childhood
like the last picture show
trying to get better
if only in his mind

of the people for the people but not really....

on dirty short d.c. streets
cement sphinx's gaze at
coition of mistakes with
garbage cans money full but
jehovah's in da house going
down america's drain
following the white rabbit's
polluted coal tar baptisms

res publica's illness is
reported serious on
twitter, drinking national kool-aid
from ayn rand's skull, we
struggle against restraints that
inhibit christian piano playing mad
souls seeking a path across the void

tortured by the furies constantly
healing in nation's asylum media
our insanity misdiagnosed as
heaven exists in hallucinations
brought on by talking points,
a pre-existing condition,
medicated red eyed harpies in
the confessional of insurance
where it takes king kong money
to put on a diaper

william burrough's ghost

dark junky streets
looking for a fix
journey in the tenement night
black eyed high hipster
up in brooklyn cold water flats
cruised college high on saroyan and ginsberg

busted on rural highways
just outside atomic city
with bags of cleaned green,
in college halls,
hammered on peyote
in that world's fair museum
in chicago's hyde park
jumping off emotional ledges

there has to be some urgency like
bullfighting in hell's kitchen
meat for the preacher
in rainy macarthur park
wandering in withering withdrawal
unstill writing arm
in empty train yards chasing
psychic mexican girls

momentarily motherless
getting it in wet barrio alleys
in winter rain looking
for bill burroughs' ghost
in the book of dreams
sentenced to jail
for juvenile intoxication
red eyed from pink catawba wine
off junk on weed

of the mind with a belly
full of olives and soul music
from broken pocket plates
tighten their watches
as to slow time left
dead on wall street
in four hundred dollar suits

unknown survivor who
jumped off michigan avenue bridge
forced to stand on the spine of the world
gather up inner cinders of thought
on broken plates in baggage rooms
souls of a thieves market
in a dream cantina
on the road of dulouz
under a new hip moon

overtaken

air, cool, dry for early november
red tailed hawk's bellies gone winter white
summer's heat a fading memory five days old
buttery shafts of sunlight filter
through gold filled autumn leaves
my waders float in murky slough water
covered in fall leaves and vibrant green duckweed
I sit an old wooden prairie farms dairy milk crate
decoys barely moving in shallow brackish water
that nurtures last surviving aquatic plants
squinting into a vibrant yellow-orange sun westing to the horizon
blue bills and teal make a furtive first pass
as they attempt the narrow path into the small island
my memories of dad and al calling hard
shutting up at just the right time
granddad telling of past storied hunts
with his father, and nine brothers
redman running a dark brown stream down their chins
lived longer than my father by nine years
still have a few good years left, maybe
tears come to my eyes staring into winter's grey sky
see their faces, hear their voices, in that foggy, autumn, moment
all feeling of being alone dissipates
ducks flair and peal off, out of range
hear dad calling me a jackass
the tears come harder

presumptive diva

rushed city voices
unmistakable elements of mockery
tuxedoed gents prowling back stages
try not to judge people
by the actions
of their state governments
themes of political seduction, submission
revolt, defeat and victory
gross tirades of gleeful discovery
spilling from bloated shadows
flowing, crawling
to no safe harbor from riots
of cross dressing acolytes
both good and bad punished
influences, inclinations drive judgment
imitative behavior unrewarded
narrative wasteland reworked
looking for new paths
allowing the presumptive diva
using the ripening insinuation
of a badly managed, bandaged, may west
causing men in six hundred dollar suits
to hurl themselves at his hem
caste roughly aside
with unmasked careless insolence
sardonic bluntness

proof reading

sun is scattering grey clouds
that make up eastern horizon
mallards and teal jump
in crisp fall air
going out to feed
in wheat colored corn
lemon sky turns to azure blue
as sun frees itself
from bare timber branches
distant doppler train horn
howls its approach
to an unmarked crossing
high tree covered bluff
just where the grist mill stood
spent lives like stiff fall leaves
thinking we are doing something
by holding on tight
when in reality we are waiting
in a constant roiling breeze
for something in the end
to arrive

Grievances

thought one day

would be able to talk to my grandchild

about duty, honor

but my mind has become my enemy

age brings on inactivity

old grievances,' fears, guilt, depression

return from the past

gnawing at me, creating doubt

fueling anxiety, igniting familiar tremors

death exists in life, war

there is a rush in killing

not unlike feeling of having survived

later, there's a debt to pay

some find it a lifelong burden

others find somehow, justification,

maybe a historical perspective, a crutch,

most, have lost part of their souls

in retrospect, I seem

to have lost my way

Undergraduates

You lost me one night in St. Louis-
came down from Chicago
drinking wine with nuns ,brakemen,
and farm girls sifting
for a Fox double feature, recklessly-
heard Waller sneer at love
looking through the hole in his head
In 1967, we were a feature in
the Lindell Boulevard, Toddle House-
I actually paid for my meal
A cowboy now and older with blake and
a cross legged ginsberg
straight out of confusion crooked
mad young gangsters
in a German Cadillac that goes narrowly
with the fiction in me-
a broken down movie extra

reading the rig veda

for some day begins at sunset
some at midnight
in a texas liquor store
some in a muddy creek bottom
on a toll road
in Indiana

never became famous
cardinal scouts watched
was just sixteen with pimples
don't remember things
faery's stole my memories

winter baby
a snowy february
grade school
in a clearing
high school
in a park
college under an arch

saying goodbye in Columbus
army with jump school
a black lotus
for a short while
lost my way

warm fourth's of july
watering thirsty tomato plants
she turned with a smile
not knowing she could do better
suffered like all do
car accidents and poverty

children two girls
strong stubborn characters
then country living
for better not worse
except for dad
leaving unexpectedly

what we experience early on
we begin to understand
getting older
not wiser
we tell of our strange dreams
surprisingly find a need to
forgive ourselves

when your voice tells you
who you are
we surprise even ourselves
and do not hesitate
to answer

silent drums (epitaph for a rock drummer)

san francisco
mid sixties
psychedelic renaissance
played free shows
on flatbed trucks
in the panhandle, golden gate park
crowds on revolutionary edge
music the foundation, catalyst
never lost the dream
community fueled by rock and roll
punctuating social distress
hard driving surreal anthems
lsd blues
music a lifting spirit
makes humanity, better even
existing outside the pale
surfers shack on mars
mad epic ideas
never stopped trying
to recreate nirvana
nothing subtle
nothing could kill him
as long the music played
to an audience that listened

sports writers

dislike *forrest gump*
solicit whores
write poetry after 60
godfather versus *good fellows*
loved *hoosiers*
natural boring
negative on designated hitter
untainted by amateur athletics
worship at Fenway and Wrigley
just take one hit
quote john wooden
having never read him
sit courtside always
high on weed
think the grave digger
was a bad coach
concerned about winning
revel other's failures
tough on their wives
and game officials
spout batshit crazy bullshit
claiming pope like infallibility

Spring 1968

May day before the rain
sunning, grazing, heartland reading
Empty sandals pointing precariously
to an open elevator door
gaping, undecided on closing-
As if it forgot purpose served and yet
wanting to let the old man in
without running heart worn gasping
Grasping for time to talk, just now
in Blue grackle flooding shade
now and then the sun soaked
Ivy, red ribbons, and barefooting silence

teacher

classroom seems a bit ordinary
student work now tattered
on cork boards thrice painted
gum coated desks
scrape marks from old circles
flag gone, holder hanging on
faded black light chalk board
holding only so much truth
so much history and doodles
desk where much was judged
coffee spilt, secrets revealed
confessions made, futures
frustrations illustrated
railing against indifference
provoking thoughts
obtuse opinion sought
retiring only when
taken for granted

tweets from your bones

get out of the way
quit facebook, twitter too
get focused on life's lyrics
short lived that
one does everything
behind a pseudonym
junkie needs to be on
with the people
not getting work done

the distractible ruins productivity
awesome for creativity
gives miracle voice soundings
ideas pulled from everywhere
neverland of connect the dots
although tantra texting
can blunt an afternoon

art needs little technology
it steels and eats ideas
mutes voice
dreams become projectiles
can't be gotten back, only
forgotten
won't let you go back
navigate the doldrums

listen to the cries
in your mind's ear
pick out the nuance of
jazzy throated thought
sounding a deep euphony
straight off the bat

process aspirations, pipe dreams
like many unique cricket clicks
say grace with meaning
no matter the situation
break down hart crane's walls
with an honesty
foundation of joy

others will weigh in
will be called out for
singing with girls for
being too cerebral
clarion for more emotion
falling in and out of wonder
at same point in time

this is more than
metaphysical break up
a snapshot, instagram, a metaphorical selfie
fathered by creative relationships whose
sons flash relationship tweets
say you can't keep it long
put it down you
don't have a choice

lake ponchartrain 1968

fifty one years ago, we drove,
eighteen hours in a march rain
through much of louisiana and mississippi
greeted by a blooded, ruddy hued cajun sky writing
over a porthole, causeway surrounded
by a grey horizonless sea

hid behind trees as
waves caught up, caste us down
storm raging, lulled
us lightening to care-
day gone and to come
ethereal sheets, eyes,
hands, hearts pumping
like mad buddhists

blossom like
forming fragile seedling foundations
trying to meet and deflect
what was almost certainly coming
holding heaven's hands in the big easy
when it meant something

in my selfish vanity
blinded by a sense of desperation
did not realize
there on canal street
you were the adult in the room
and I the child

white power

small town burger joint
slick black back booths on
white tiled squares
dark cigarette stains
going up corners of mouths
midnight drinkers escort
fat women in red silk with
gold ring fingers
like a drunken burlesque
inebriated by the smell of creosote
and the essence of wood
stained in kerosene
a fat nosed girl dances
with a hip mexican
with sideburns like elvis
on a scary creaking wooden floor
standing on the back of the world
in a gas lamp alley
leading to the switchman's sordid shack,
one can look into their eyes,
these dark archaeologists,
and see the backs of their skulls

Marijuana
  Dream

On any ancient day
I sit down and try
to remember the future
as I thought it was going to be-
wakeful madras nights
listening to a transistor radio
tying life in rock and roll paisley knots
misconceptions baby fed
soft core soda fountain promises
love thought forever
like in those beat teen movie magazines
or in that low slow Detroit soul sound
bodies of great purpose purloined
quarried by blue jeaned Buddhists
ornaments of life's corporality
putting apostles in handcuffs
getting high on nothing

exercise yard

out there in the exercise yard
in the county jail
on stark concrete wall
perched among the black marks
made by inmates
working out frustrations
playing handball
a monarch butterfly rests
slowly opening and closing its wings
yard is open only to the sky
finds inmates, felons and murderers,
begging female guard
to capture it and release it
outside the jail's walls
being ever so careful not to hurt it
to set it free
in a collective of hope
that they one day join the fragile inmate
outside the shadow of chain link

veterans day

not saying there shouldn't be
a veteran's day-
state cons people
a day, moments
of silences, patriotic
broken track driver, corpsman,
boy from Columbus loved
by that skinny catholic girl,
mass graves done for
body counting that mother
face down in the paddy
seemingly reaching blindly
for children who never found her
old men with orange livers failing
a grateful nation is
just not enough

West Pine Alumni

I lived on West Pine just west of Grand
fourth floor northeast corner Clemens-
Big room enough for three with the Roman couch maybe four
labored, a student, as a failed poet,
frightened choir boy looking to basic training-
helped each other through sickness, ruptured arteries,
lost, spurned loves, and those fun ambulance rides- but
at the end we lost each other and ourselves
in the establishment's stockyard reality that
innocent mad life replaced by a war, grad school,
drugs, and love-the culture we created
more fragile than imagined—in just
one day it was gone

gravity

walking to class one day
on those soaked wet sidewalks
on west pine
strained sore eyes water filled
did find hope and common foundation
so fragile it broke like thin cheap china
slowly in bits and pieces of 1960's reality
like a kerouac crossing mentality that
in the next decade, wandering lost,
on platform shoes and wide collars
flowers ripped from soft hands
somewhere in san francisco
or in a village coffee house
the magic dragon lost
to the establishment
all of us now
poets of the night

hurricane

sitting in a hotel room
on upper east side
coffee cup in hand
wearing green overcoat
stockings with fashionable holes in them
cropped bleach blond
remembering sandy
a zombie apocalypse
panicked people falling,
kicking each other to the pavement
when the lights go out
civilization fails with it
this brooks brothers buddhism
warming up to midnight
in weaving mass of shadows
walking down the bishop's way
on whispering gravel
far off sound of bell buoy
shifting on its' moorings
marking time like a metronome
measuring limits of constraint
in what we believe
and what is the truth

making music

in a hilltop cottage
in stinson beach
cooked dinner together
walked on the beach
sometimes sharing a joint
no one for miles
like being inside the sky
stars and planets
right next to your eyes
something special flowed there
spilling out and stopping
life beating you down
changing, morphing to stay happy
avoiding destructive relationships
vicious cycles of lost creativity
taking song fragments
stringing them together
a time to sow
staying away from Nashville
its dumbing down of the music
glorifying the uneducated and racist
apocalyptic mind control

maycomb

saying in the south
want two baptist churches
build the first
wait for the break-a-way

south has strong ties
to church and property
not carpetbagger greed for land
but for what makes a home

a sick sister in eufaula
solace of a catfish pond
using hot dogs for bait
bobbers leaving few ripples

sweet tea is civilized
baskets of fried oysters
sweet potato rounds
sawmill gravy and quaker plain

a fierceness and independence
exists in the southern tradition of storytelling
roots both celtic and african
that appreciates beauty without possessing it

a table at radley's in monroeville
or one in stockton at the stage coach café
bread crumbed fish fried lightly
like being in high cotton

played in woods as a child
no real respect for rules
except set by high school english teacher
like a creek indian journey proud

feeding quarters into the machines
at the excel laundromat
working weight off
from melvin's barbeque on cherry street

best days in memory
always linger with a sound, a scent
feeding ducks in late afternoon
occurrence of mockingbird in nelle lee's yard

change has come at a cost
shop's owner calling you by name
at darby's red and white
lost interactions of the general store

in burnt corn, finchburg, and scratch ankle
where it's correct to say "cheese grits is"
like the two hundred year old oak in uriah
dody still listens to atticus on the front porch swing

millennials

venus rocks
in white denim
in the bowery
did the apple juice jump
drank signature cocktails
marked a tortured back-story
with self-guided tours
getting back to
what they do best
anger, brooding, depression
this is the batshit version
of god playing guitar
trying to find sobriety
in a break between spirit and body
tried working construction
but was sacked after three weeks
now in the twitter age
with a bottle of patron in hand
and a tenor sax in the other
sporting a flat top
wing like shoulder pads
hear it every day in the barbershop
sitting there like hollywood squares
passionate, inspired, original
eternal sunshine of a glue huffer
sons of music teachers
know that the future is leaving
nothing to relate to
having to walk home alone
on seedy barrio nights
looking for a persian rug with cherubs
while face down in bong water

moon in a henri rousseau painting

hipsters broken down
river rats
ministers rolled up
sleeves, surfers, greasers on
big Mississippi river night in
mad saint george room
all friends after six
always suspicious
of being completely trusting
ten dollar buckets
goths on a break
bird dogs in a box
evangelical's god chasers
plying everything
not their wives
with no real belief
songs doggedly sung
with a constant bored refrain
searching in the smoky dim light
to reason some sanity
all eyes on the door waiting
for the messiah to come in
all the time messiah sitting
on the bar stool next to them

muse

sometimes
i get to writing
with good intent
actually going somewhere
along the way
the mind plays a trick
off to some mad place
creation, go with it
original destination crackback
images jump out
metaphors bend and twist
makes you feel
like a carnival barker
a mad hatter fraud
passing my own surprise
onto the leaves
a rural country road
explored in my youth
each bend brings odyssey
evolving into
all that we are
all which is to come
no control
just the self
trying to guide me
somewhere I have never been

national anthem

turned them down
he did
asked him to masquerade
as a war hero

daily he fights alienation
from his former self
his ghost past makes
a misfit at home

disengaged public
finds war wildly popular
at sporting events somehow
finding themselves undeserving of the effort

with every bar sung
mind is reopened
every pat on the back makes
you want to burn everything down

history distorts war
authors work well
to find plot and meaning
sorting out the fragmentation

there is not enough room
for what is brought home
and no one seems to know
what he is being thanked for

normal heart

day has a playlist
heartfelt grooves
breaks creative logjams
highlights emotional flaws
infield errors honored
as hidden intentions
sing into sadness
canons of life
makes a tasty soul

write catchy tune,
about nerve induced asthma attack
don't miss a beat
wage a heavy peace as
going around corners gets scary
see it with new dead eyes
get into woodworking
follow hockey in church basements
crush the black capsule

life is a godzilla disaster movie
success beats you down
tough to imagine
ever being young
an original american horror story
billionaires in birkenstocks
johnny cash not being played
on country radio
teenage jesus jerks in cowboy hats

creative people don't always turn out
to be interesting
like chance meetings in london tube
someone called amy
conversation like watching sausage
and politics being made
world just gets tinier
it used to be a stage
a private confessional

on returning to st. louis

every visit
memories crawl out
from the shadows of buildings
pulls me into the neighborhood
of west pine and sarah
the same spring smells
jar stored memories in vision
at professional hockey game
search the crowd for familiar faces
correct myself, forgetting my age
for looking at younger faces
force myself to look
for bald guys and white hair
finding them in the foyers
drinking beer in circles
with same easy going mentality
that seems part of my past
this city pulls on me
when I try to leave
and when I'm there
part of me is lost and frantic
like returning to a house
you once lived in
familiar and again a stranger
people made it what it was
now they are gone also
the city is what it is
that world is lost forever
but the memories mine to keep

paradox

no one wins
black comedy of history
rising candidates further the abyss
crazy or too bumbling
like henry the second
king of Jerusalem
fell to his death
in the arms of a dwarf
kissing every local ass
like citizens united
performing on life support
cracking rubber jokes
processed sociopathic liars
all bad actors with dog whistles
historically two hundred years old
right wing religious gangbangers
folding up american dream
on a government credit card
driven by a novelty act
realism a non copacetic
no brilliant planks here
like dents on a Mercedes
trumped up hale woman
screaming at a printer
producing facile images
imagined mined embryos
just three pages
taxed and bleeding out resisting
cameras always on
ratings through odin's gate
dark horses, physician healing himself
migrant drones crossing borders

played third base for hell's angels
trying to be more unhinged than the next
filling old cheops with political grain
at a point most repeatedly mad
that some begin to inevitably believe
it is the most reasonable course

parmita dana (*perfection of clarity*)

greatest power of the mind
seeing what's not there
mystery of making things up
a cowboy on a horse
a lab named spot

doing best with nonexistent deadlines
mad hatter dinner at seven, be there
bring face painted flowers,
too conventional,
bring antique standing mirror,
any house can use another

bring a book
books stay quiet
when you want to think
except one missing
last page

leave the windows open
so your music and I
can converse
gives the moonlight
something worth shining on

a warm breeze that comes
with gentle rain as
elfin ears hear
different soft whispers
every night
real life doesn't measure up
to imagination

pencil sharpener

one night I began
looking, a quest
for a pencil sharpener
like the kids have at school

I ventured into
my daughters' old desks
long derelict
girls are away now
desks tinned like shrines

opening drawers took me back
through their childhoods
erasers in heart and bear shapes
old baseball cards we got together
pencils, lots, never used
old school notes
college application forms
valentines from boys
pictures marking milestones
athletic awards
college letters from coaches
books we read together
unlocking vivid memories forgotten

all started looking for a sharpener
because those pencils
unsharpened , blunted, abandoned
helped my perspective, not of their departure, my loss
but the gift of their lives
to share in their ongoing experiences

like their first steps, first day of school
graduations, jobs, husbands,
my grandchildren
student loans

universities in bed
with banks with gold
stars for sale
measured by the weight
watchers walk uptown
passed blurred caste lines
dying by a thousand cuts
forever without rem sleep
rodents for friends
like taking stage
after metallica
like karaoke after chernobyl,
torpedoes and wildflowers, wearing
mick jagger's cape
studded collar sneakers just
back from samoan exile
in a cheap chicago spy bar
creative boundaries limitless
freebasing, speedball, accelerants
in hotel hooker hookahs
shoot out god's light
this life no recital
get ready for a brand new beat
it's existence, minus the stupid
not the one that got away

ptsd

vampire like constant sorrow
feeding on the lonely
snatching what's left of boyhood
like going back to baghdad
at a fork in the path
trying to come on strong
awkwardly brilliant
these dirty damn humans
hotter than hell
damaged goods, rude
can't hide from your experience
like attending a fly's funeral
in a hyde park riot
no more romantic figures
takes one to a dark place
in the womb of the state
you come out fighting
but you can't come back
flashbacks won't let you

scout lee

our country's culture
grown coarse and obscene
has distanced itself from a time
when railroad tracks connected
things that mattered
like one generation to the next
language is no longer a play
post-its went to tweets
nation's fierceness
independence now gone
predictable as noon bells
like an indulged childhood
of a southern goddess
it roils in Mississippi mud
lost is sound of ice
clinking in glass of ice tea
it was civilized
quality met quality
it meant you were "pourin"
made you feel cooler
from smut eye in bullock county
to otter creek in macoupin
once journey proud
standing in high cotton no more
pounding the preacher
or the poser
dancing in the eye
of a man made hurricane

sleeping sycamores

in the early waxing quarter moon
like the snap of a heavy bottom branch
a heavy cast church bell sounds an unbroken stark clarion
cutting silence like a dull scissors
erasing the peace
like a rock to a windshield

frost has padlocked the orchard
only caramel colored, apple mummies remain
late fall is nature's sleeping pill
just before snow brings its harlequin mask
and frost glazes antediluvian glass
with its own self-portrait

time of late night book lights
magnified by whisky filled shot glasses
and creaking old house timbers
old eyes roll over written lines
until early dawn strikes a mental key
casting first die of the new day

as life endeavors to bid
card hands to be played
backhands to be practiced
letters to be written
traditions to be broken
more books to be read

southside hardware

came to fix the pump
check the furnace
change in line filters
in the old farm house
down in otter creek bottom
greenfield boys come unannounced
because she forgets to call
at door of dugout basement
just under the threshold
small massasauga rattler
trying to get out of a cold fall rain
woman in her nineties
brushes snake away with her cane
little one she says
gingerly armed with flashlights
down they go eyes searching at their feet
not for leaks but for momma

suicide at owl creek farm

valley just outside aspen
put a pistol to his head
was frightfully drunk, on drugs
incited mayhem like
huffing ether outside vegas
gonzo journalist
experiencing the truth
manic life force
cavorting with surreal actors

liked his guns
threatened to shoot everyone
marched through doors in woody creek
shotgun leveled at bartender
shooting blanks
setting off smoke bombs
clearing the place
liked his tequila
drank everything
but never wine
couldn't get cork out of bottle

creeks there run hard
laden with trout in spring
as new colts get their legs
drugs and booze
part of the american dream
pushing people's buttons
used a cannon over owl creek
to spread his ashes
fishing was good that spring

synthesis

excised synthetic sweat
in a shot glass
perspiration of cage fighters, lovers
somehow collected at climax
using gas chromatography
viscous yellow, slightly disgusting
physical representation, sex and aggression
entirely manufactured, counterfeit
ambiguous to nature
like stiletto heels, bullets, drones
form follows no function
like a gun made on a 3-d printer

maybe like the rapture
age of design is upon us
likened behavior made of video games
brings pacman to picasso
leaving no tangible evidence of peace
no longer the need to possess
acquisition acknowledges existence
changes perspective about
ethics of design
old temples are crumbling
we are designing our own gods

terry pratt

we sat the same bench
in that july all star game
both of us
young bold bragging
like chattering jay birds
both legends
in our own minds
talked of playing
in the majors
scouts there that night
he threw a baseball
four hundred feet
to a base almost effortlessly
caught him for three innings
he was throwing 90 at sixteen
homered behind me to tie
loved any contest
to show off that arm
died in vietnam in '68
see him still
head cocked back
hands in front pockets
of his faded jeans
making fun of everyone
and himself
holding a coke bottle
half full of peanuts
asking if I wanted to race
he'd give me a headstart
to the park and back
fifty years later
bought a round

at the legion hall
in his memory
and to mine

tomahawk

think about it no more than five
or six hours a day
never goes away
failing seven out of ten times
makes for success

cell phones take up
all the rest of the available space
to the exclusivity
of a more than personal life

took a six year old
left her there
everything is alright
if we just don't talk about it

she thought
she had done something wrong
never was a time or place
things drift and lines blur

he couldn't give her
what she wanted
he gave her
what she needed

gave his blood
to give her sunshine
name on the door
single malt drunk from the bottle

he gave her his voice
ornament from a father
kept his problems to himself
kept hers at bay

troubadour

doesn't own a smart phone or a laptop
gets his email in the library
in gallop new mexico
along with eleven navajos
searches antique stores in springfield
for old country seventy eights
looking for regional treasures
old front man for
a spoon river jug band
playing dixie truck stops,
chatauquas, and church carnivals
sometimes just to prairie dogs
and stars in colorado

sipping old taylor
from a paper cup
scribbling songs in between
life's narrow lines
long ago ignored
apocalyptic predictions of failure
mining myths, lies and loves of
tobacco chewing tragic lives
shabby carnival barkers looked down on
for what they seem
hillbillies, ridge runners, preacher's kids
america's native sons and daughters

writing songs that sing
in long abandoned steel rails
playing banjo with wide eyed students
on southern college campus's
harvesting cranberries in maine
running white lightning in tennessee

selling weed in twenty three dollar a night motels
drinking whiskey without eating
doesn't equal out trying to be balanced
like a single drop of rain
trying to put a name on the influences
on the music he plays at life

waiting on a rollercoaster

it takes godzilla money
hiding in plain sight
crowds bring on
panic attacks started
with doing shakespeare

a beatnik jew
from long island
desparate always
to be alive
spray paint childhood
stolen car dreams
no security
in real love

never learned boundaries
anger focused wildly
on those loved
haven't dreamt in years
fights about everything
has what he has
born from being deprived

loving old things
classical music
black and white movies
likes them because
he is the only one
who likes them

corn flower blue eyes
a galaxy away from
lower east side
squatting in abandoned buildings
forgetting looks a lot
like happiness separated
from memories
as deep as tombs

Waste Hauler

Dean remembered
being stranded just
outside North Platte
Called it the last green place
before the waste
of the grazing lands
smell of cattle and animal rot

Imagine riding
straight line from
Omaha to Cheyenne
at 70 miles an hour
on a flatbed trailer
holding on to a brace chain
trying to piss off the back
To relieve oneself
of the past

water woman

navajo route six sixty-six
west of shiprock
east of redstone
just below old sheep enclosure
in san juan river bottom
north of that hard road
farm buildings, recent construction
seem out of place
deep well there with old hand pump
handle faces west
frozen upright
by lightening strike
night the old woman died

lived up that way
used to walk her stock to the creek
hogs, cattle, few sheep
they followed her
she died on that stretch of road
just to the east
just at the hill's crest
just one day after
her ninety-first birthday

wreath there
on the no passing sign
constantly replaced over the years
she haunts that creek bottom
echoes of her calling off
in morning mists
sends chills out to those who hear
still draws current stock
to the shallow hard running water

william faulkner's rocking chair

oxford
a southern college town
quiet antebellum square
except on football weekends
fellow at the blind pig said
real mississippi starts fifty miles south
of rowan oak's drive

nielson's full of fine sundries
corner bar thrives but
at the corner bookstore
on the second floor full
of old books on hand made shelves
is bill faulkner's pine rocking chair

an uninterested lady clerk
barely looks up and
goes back to her scented candles and notions
perhaps a member, the white goddess cult
in good standing

up some sparse hand hewn stairs
roped off next to a florence wood stove
chairs arranged in no order
some cained some leather back
where for some years he sat at coffee
with intransigent friends
and northern interventionists

exploring gender and class
often conflicted by
inherited pernicious beliefs
with insight and sympathy later
not common of his time

on that very perch sat I
no permission sought
no eyes to see
conversed with ghosts
without sound and
with no fury

About the Poet

Dan Jacoby, a former educator, steel worker and Army Special Forces, is a graduate of St. Louis University, Chicago State University, and Governors State University. He has published poetry *in Anchor and Plume(Kindred), Arkansas Review, Belle Reve Literary Journal, Bombay Gin, Burningword Literary Review, Canary, The Fourth River, Wilderness House Literary Review, Steel Toe Review, The American Journal of Poetry*, and *Red Fez* to name a few. He is a member of the Carlinville Writers' Guild and was nominated for a Pushcart Prize in 2015.